MARRIAGE AND FAMILY PROBLEMS PROFILE

LEWIS DONALD KITE, Ph.D.

GRAPH
Publishing, L.L.C.

Published by
GRAPH Publishing, L.L.C.
www.graphpublishing.com

Printed in the U.S.A.

TABLE OF CONTENTS

ABOUT THE AUTHOR

LEWIS DONALD KITE, Ph.D.

Lewis Donald Kite is the President of Kite Laboratories, Inc. in Houston, Texas. He has formally served as professor of Psychology, NASA subcontractor, and medical laboratory director. At the present, he also provides consulting services to medical professionals in the field of psychiatry.

Dr. Kite received international recognition when he published a paper showing that aspirin is effective in the prevention and treatment of strokes and other vascular disorders. He is a biochemist, mental health professional, medical researcher, and inventor.

Dr. Kite has earned a doctorate in psychology as well as certificates in Art Therapy, Addictionology, Crisis Intervention Stress Management, Hypnotherapy, Neuro-Linguistic Programming, and faith-based counseling. In addition, he has completed six years of postgraduate study in analytical psychology.

Dr. Kite's inventions and tests in medicine and psychology include prescription and non-prescription medications, the Nine Item Symbolic Profile, The Harm Potential Profile, the Sexual Problems Identification Profile, and the Marriage and Family Problems Identification Profile.

Dr. Kite is available for Test Interpretations, Patient Evaluations and Counseling Assistance in regards to Test Results. He may be contacted for hire at the following:

KITE LABORATORIES, Inc.

Dr. Lewis Donald Kite, Ph.D.

Email: ldkite@aol.com

INTRODUCTION

This profile is an adjunct to the therapeutic process and is designed to help psychiatrists, other physicians, social workers, other licensed mental health professionals, counselors, and ministers to identify difficulties of persons with marital or family problems.

The **Marriage and Family Problems Profile** provides an insight into the patient's subconscious mind and uncovers problem areas beyond the person's awareness. The profile consists of the "**Ruth Fry Symbolic Profile**" and the "**Nine Item Symbolic Profile**" and "**Family Profile**".

Our **Marriage and Family Problems Profile** was developed after years of study of art therapy, analytical psychology, and psychoanalysis. It is our sincere hope that you will utilize this profile to effectively identify and treat people with marital and family problems.

THE RUTH FRY SYMBOLIC PROFILE

The Ruth Fry Symbolic Profile has been a valuable counseling aid for over thirty years.

The profile quickly identifies the patient's problems.

There are no right or wrong responses to the profile.

The Ruth Fry Symbolic Profile—Instructions for administration to patients:

1. First, give the patient a copy of page 10 "Ruth Fry Symbolic Profile." Instruct the patient to draw a picture in each of the boxes of the profile using the symbols in the boxes on pages 11 through 16. Then instruct them to label each box in the profile, naming the picture they drew using the specified symbols.

2. Second, when this exercise is completed, instruct the patient to complete each sentence on page 18 with quick, first responses.

THE RUTH FRY SYMBOLIC PROFILE

Name_____   Date_____

Sex_____   Age_____

Marital status: M S D W

Directions:

1. Draw something in each square below using the symbol presented. Label each square.
2. After the pictures are completed, finish the sentences on the next pages using the key words with a quick, first response.

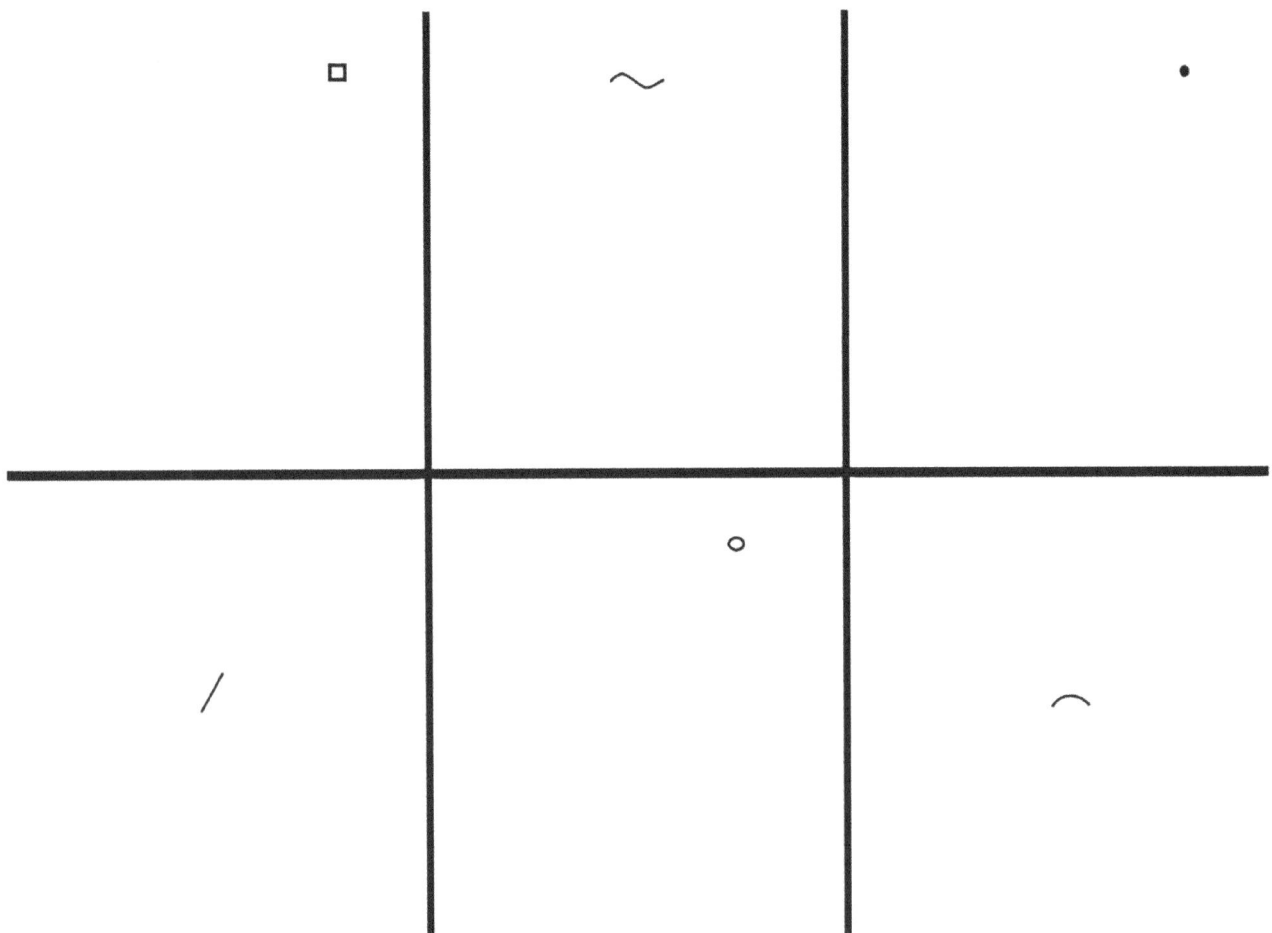

EGO SQUARE

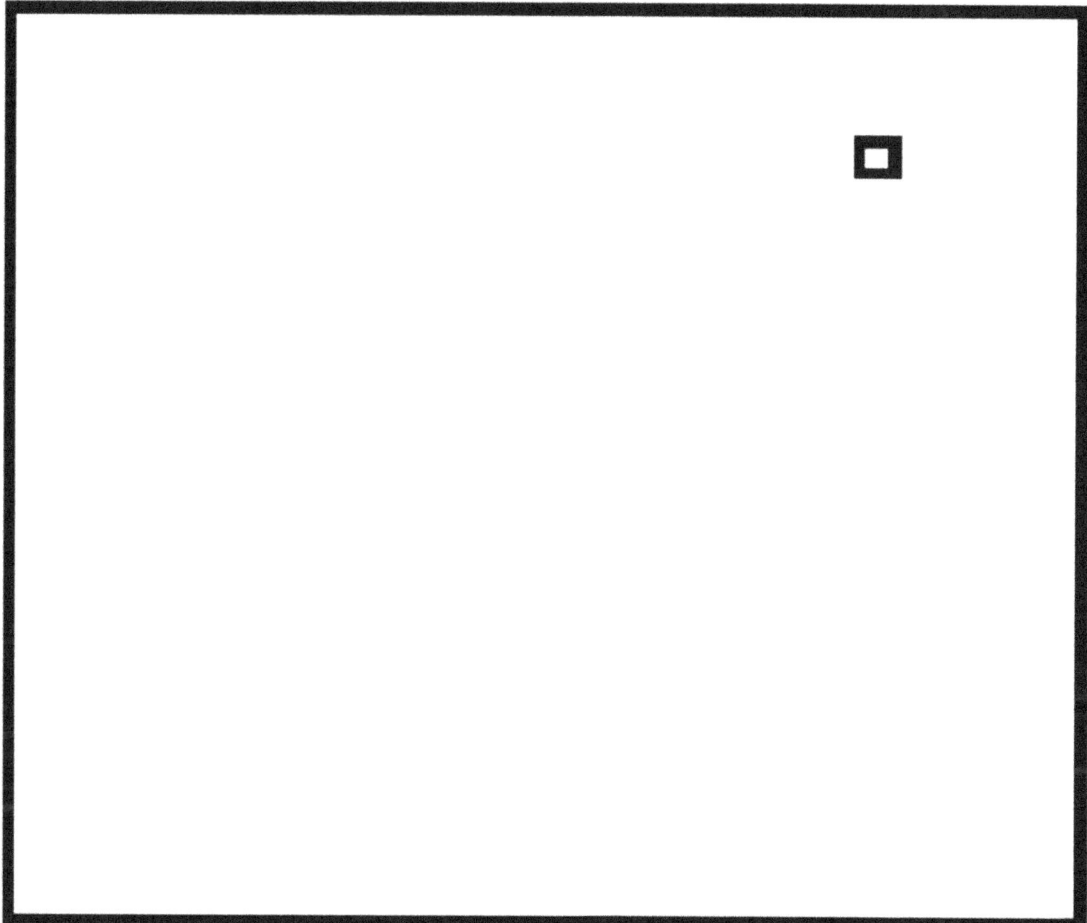

The "EGO" symbol in square #1 elicits from the unconscious of the person drawing the picture thoughts about what he or she thinks and feels about him/herself and his or her self-image. Symbols of death in this square indicate a desire to commit suicide.

"The symbol in the Ego Square (#1) is the quaternary, a small square, an earth form, having to do with the maternal and passive. The ego forms the center of the field of consciousness, and in so far as this comprises the empirical personality, the ego is the subject of all personal acts of consciousness. The Ego is the means by which adaptation to outward reality is experienced." (Fry, 1976)

FANTASY SQUARE

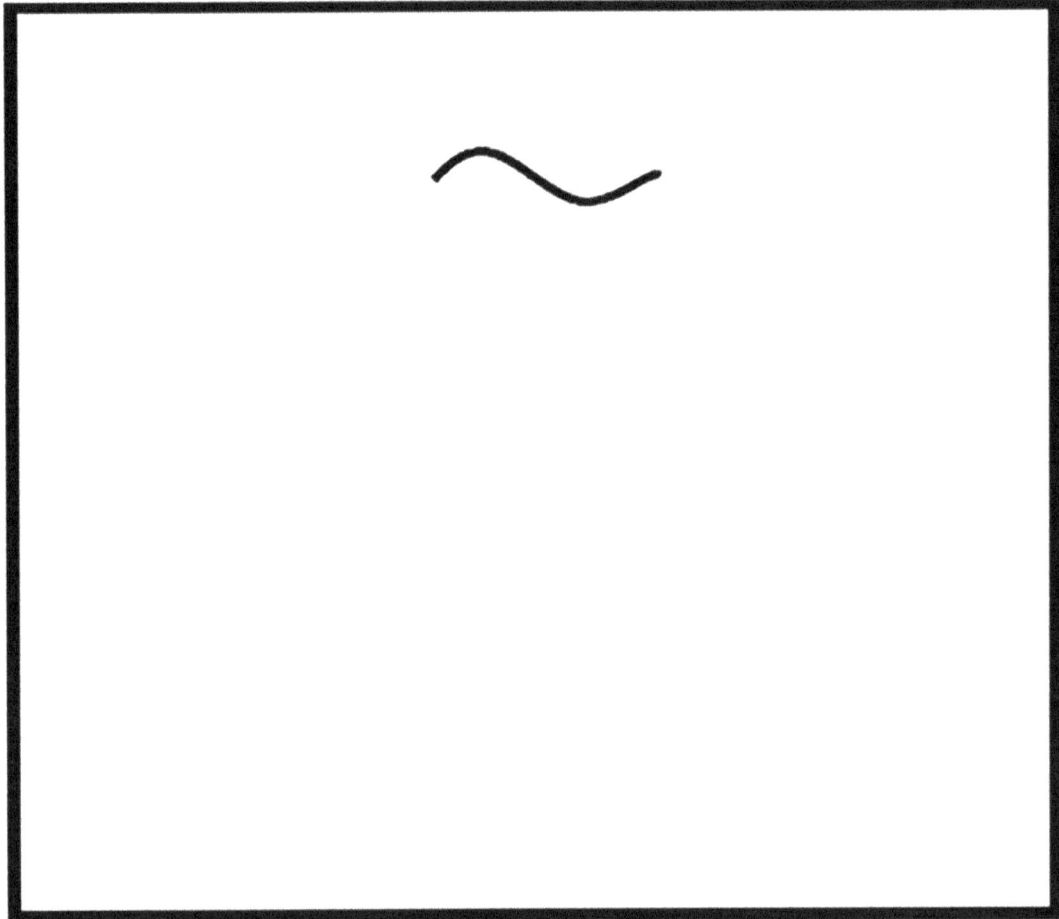

~

The "FANTASY" symbol in square #2 elicits fantasies from the unconscious mind of the person. The drawing represents the fantasy life of the individual and what he/she would like to do or be. Symbols of death in this picture indicate a fantasy to commit suicide.

"The wavy line in the Fantasy Square (#2) is a symbol of air and could represent imaginative thoughts or ideas floating around, or the possibilities of solutions which are still up in the air. These would be elusive, indefinite contents of the unconscious." (Fry, 1976)

FAMILY SQUARE

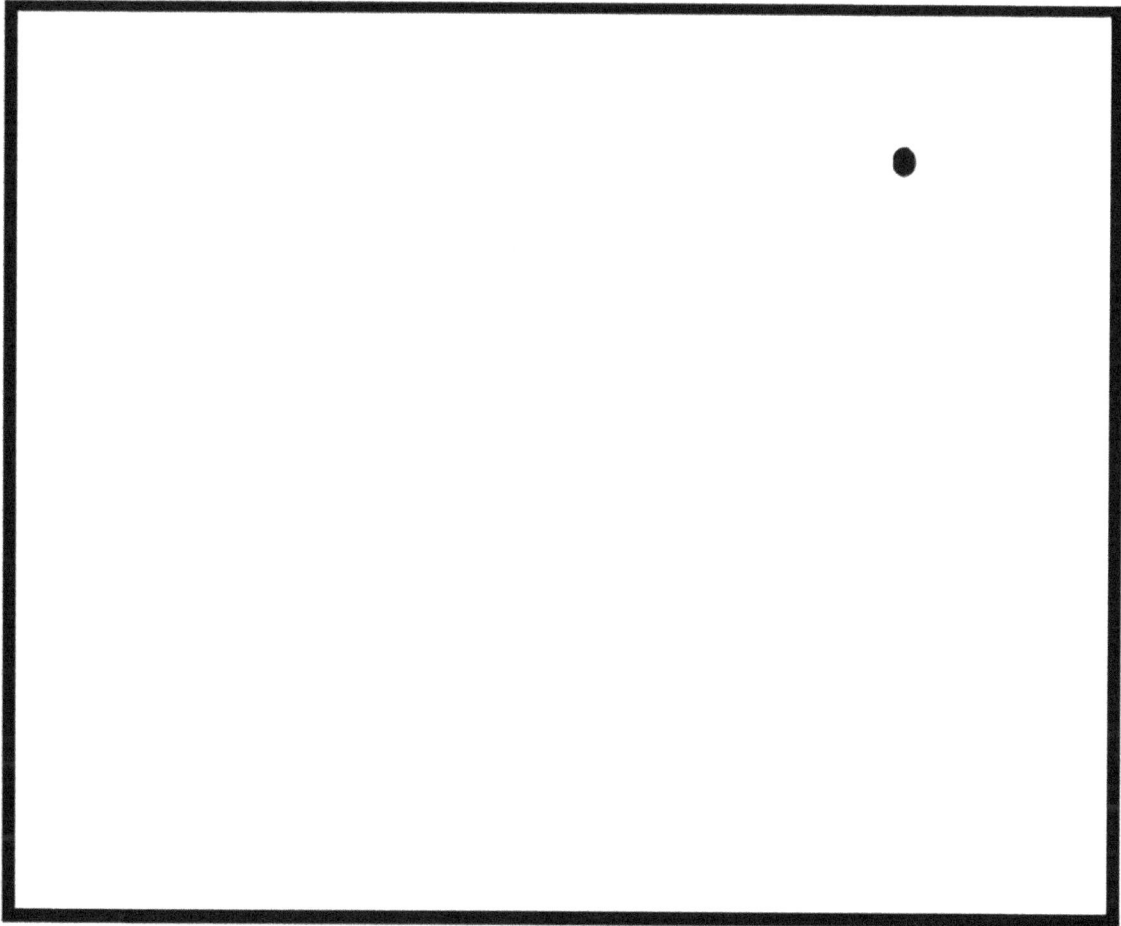

The "FAMILY" symbol, #3, elicits from the unconscious mind of the person drawing the picture thoughts about his or her family and about the relationship to his/her family. The patient expresses his/her place in the family and the relationship to his/her family. Symbols of death in the picture are an indication of the person harming members of his/her family.

"The 'unity of origin' symbol, a small dot, is in the Family Square (#3). The family is the most instinctive, fundamental social, or mating, group—the seed of individual origin. This social unit is the first place in which we begin to experience ourselves in relationship to others." (Fry, 1976)

SELF-DETERMINATION SQUARE

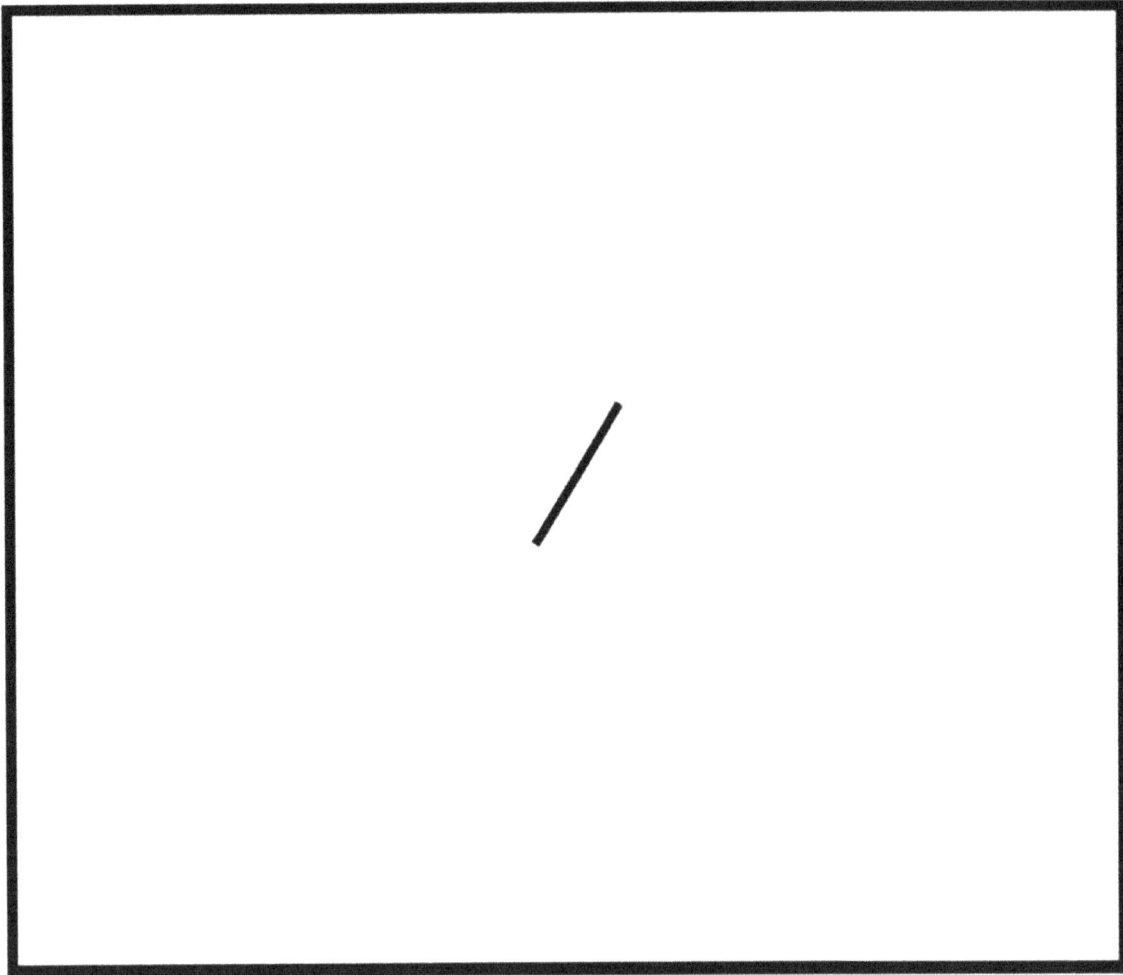

The "SELF-DETERMINATION" symbol in square #4 elicits from the unconscious the patient's aspirations and how he/she wants to change him/herself. Symbols of death in this picture indicate a determination to commit suicide.

"The Self-Determination Square (#4) with the diagonal line contains the symbol for the 'active dynamic principle.' The development of the diagonal line would be an indication of the person's search for direction in life." (Fry,1976)

RELIGION SQUARE

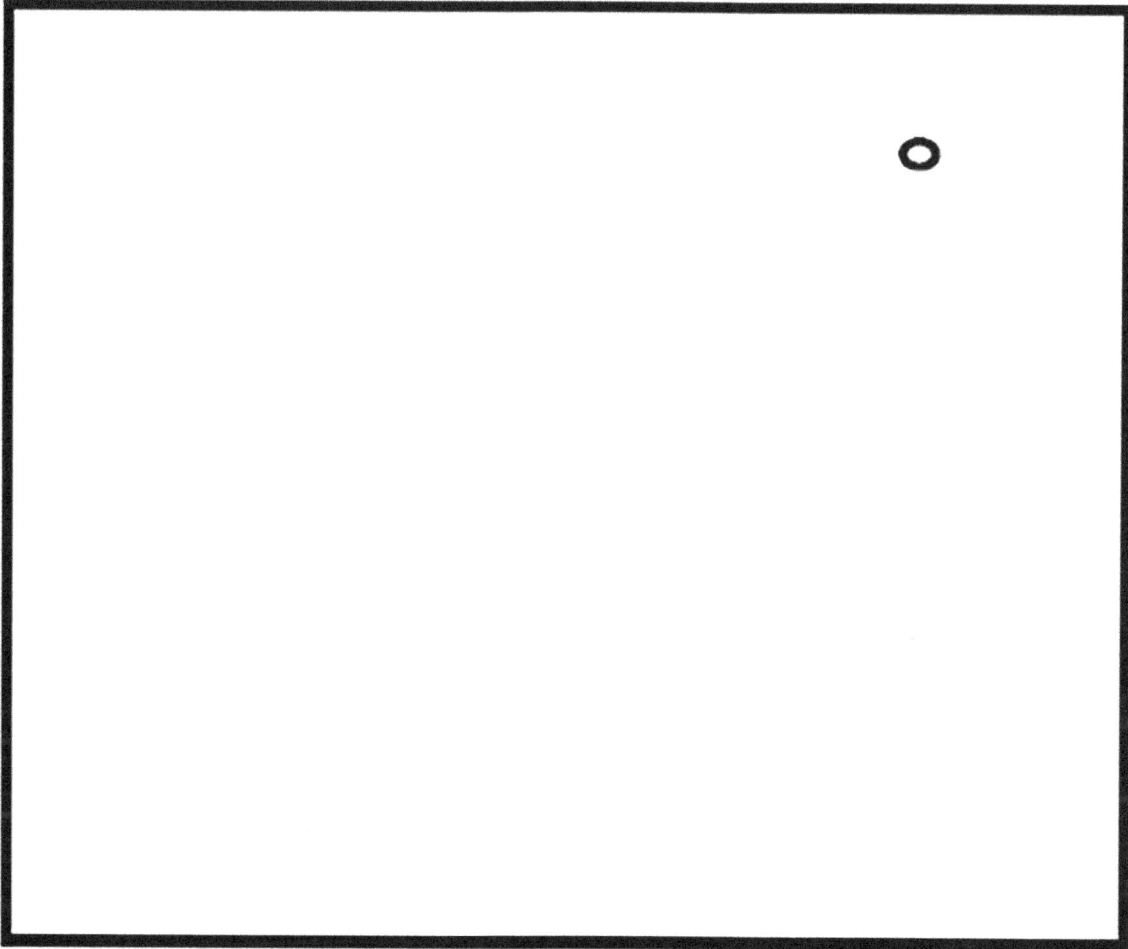

The "RELIGION" symbol in square #5 elicits from the unconscious what the person thinks about religion and God.

"The symbol in the Religion Square (#5) represents infinity, the universe, the Almighty. The symbol would help to express the universal, instinctive need to be in touch with that which is more than we. The relationship, or lack of relationship, to a god-image, either personal or impersonal, is where we seek the ultimate meaning of life. From our perception of this image, reflecting life's meaning, we derive our ethical behavior and/or moral attitudes." (Fry, 1976)

POTENTIAL SQUARE

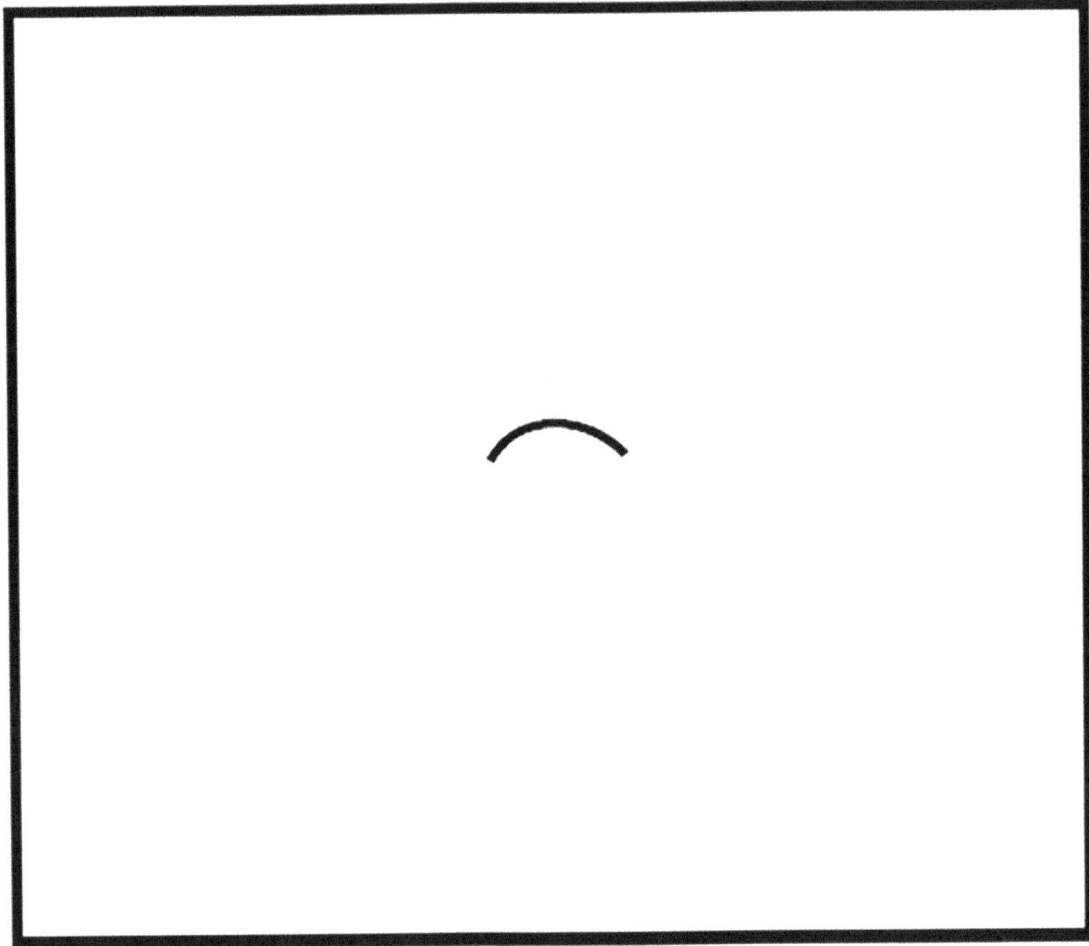

The "POTENTIAL" symbol, #6, elicits from the unconscious what the patient thinks will become of him/her in the future. Symbols of death in the picture indicate future plans for violence.

"The arc in the Potential Square (#6) is part of a circle. The circle symbolizes wholeness, denotes the totality of the personality. The symbol is left open on the profile for the purpose of stimulating the person to find his/her own potential." (Fry, 1976)

SENTENCE COMPLETIONS

The sentence completions can be utilized by the counselor to identify the problems, desires, feeling, and relationships of the patient.

Each sentence can be matched up with one of the corresponding pictures according to their content and should be considered in counseling. For example, the person may have several sentences referring to relationships with family members that correspond to their Family Square (#3). Get the person to talk about their sentence completions, and have them relate them to their drawing in the appropriate square.

Don't overlook the good things in the person's life that they note in the sentence completions. One technique that works wonders is to discuss at the end of each session one of the good things that the person likes that he or she disclosed in the sentence completions. This helps the person to get back to enjoying life by fiving the person something else to think about.

Discussing something good in the person's life will also make them want to return for further counseling. It only takes a few minutes at the end of each session to discuss with the person what they like or love.

We also are including a Problem Areas Sheet Form with our profile, so you can list problem areas and good things to talk about in therapy. This should be an important part of your treatment plan for each person.

SYMBOLIC PROFILE SENTENCE COMPLETIONS

1. I like _____
2. I want _____
3. My family _____
4. I must _____
5. Church is _____
6. I hope _____
7. I love _____
8. I feel _____
9. Children are _____
10. People think of me _____
11. God _____
12. I often _____
13. I hate _____
14. Someday I _____
15. My father _____
16. I cannot _____
17. I fear _____
18. I wish _____
19. I failed _____
20. My greatest success _____
21. My mother _____
22. I need _____
23. I believe _____
24. My worst fault _____
25. Women _____
26. Love _____
27. Sisters are _____
28. I regret _____
29. I was happiest when _____
30. People _____
31. Men _____
32. Sex _____
33. At home _____
34. I miss _____
35. I think _____
36. Marriage _____
37. Brothers _____
38. A spouse _____
39. I think of myself as _____
40. My dreams _____

THE FAMILY PORTRAIT

The Family Portrait, developed by H. Kwiakowska, is a commonly used assessment tool in art therapy. Each person is asked to draw a picture of their family.

The goal of the therapist is to get each of the family members to represent their problems in art, to bring out the feelings about their problems, and to find a solution to their problems. The therapist gets each member of the family group involved in helping to analyze and interpret the art of each of the other members, thus getting a perspective on how the other members of the family feel about the problems and their possible solutions to them.

USE OF THE FAMILY PORTAIT IN MARRIAGE COUNSELING

I.   Administer the Family Portrait to both marital partners and have each draw a picture of both of them and label the picture.

II.   Notice how each client draws themself and their spouse. For example, if ears are absent in the drawing of a marital partner, it indicates that the person doesn't listen to the other partner.

III.   Ask each person to talk about their own picture and help analyze and interpret their pi cure.

IV.   Ask each marital partner to help analyze and interpret the picture their marital partner draws.

V.   Utilize the information you obtain from the profiles to help develop a treatment plan.

VI.   Administer the Family Portrait at different stages of the therapy to check the progress of the couple.

USE OF THE FAMILY PORTRAIT IN FAMILY THERAPY

I.   Administer the Family Portrait to each of the family members and have each of them draw a picture of themselves and their family members and label each person.

II. Which family members are closest to the client in the pictures? Closeness indicates emotional closeness.

III. Which family members are farthest away from the client in the picture? Those farthest away may indicate emotional separation.

IV. Notice how the client draws each figure. That is how the client sees each person in the family. For example, a figure without ears might indicate that the person doesn't listen to the client. The picture of the client without ears indicates the client doesn't listen to their family.

V.   Have the client describe the scene in their own profile and describe and talk about each family member.

VI. Have each family member analyze and interpret the pictures of each of the other family members.

VII. Re-administer the Family Portrait to each of the family members later on in therapy to check the progress of the couple.

THE FAMILY PORTRAIT

Name _____

Date _____

Sex _____

Age _____

Directions:

1. Draw a picture of you and your family members below.

2. Label the picture of each person with their name.

THE NINE ITEM SYMBOLIC PROFILE

The Nine Item Symbolic Profile, developed by Dr. Lewis D. Kite, is an adjunct to the therapeutic process. It has been utilized successfully by mental health professionals to identify persons with sexual problems and other problems. The profile consists of nine symbols that the person uses to draw a picture with all the symbols as part of the picture. The drawing uncovers:

1. Interpersonal relationships
2. Attitudes toward sex
3. Attitude toward the person's body
4. Relationship to the parents
5. Attitude toward the environment the person is in
6. The person's career and future
7. The person's defenses
8. The person's relationship to God
9. The self

INSTRUCTIONS FOR ADMINISTRATION

1. Give the person a copy of the profile and instruct them to draw a picture utilizing all of the symbols listed as part of the picture.

ANALYSIS OF THE PROFILE
Look for the following:

TREE SYMBOLISM:

1. Knot hole in the tree — This indicates sexual abuse.

2. Blackened hole in the tree — Indicates shame associated with the sexual encounter.

3. Absence of leaves in tree (dead tree) — Indicates the need for sex, but no desire or capacity to give affection.

4. Heavy lines drawn in tree — This indicates anger and hostility with love or sex.

POND SYMBOLISM: Symbolizes the parent of the opposite sex

1. Size of pond — The larger the size, the larger the influence the parent had on the person.

2. Pond on right side of drawing — This indicates they are saying the parent was right.

3.   Pond on left side od drawing — This indicates that the person is saying the parent was wrong.

4.   Waves in pond — This usually indicates some type of conflict with the parent.

5.   Shading in the pond picture — This indicates bad feelings about the parent.

6.   Vegetation in the pond — This indicates bad feelings about the parent.

7.   Ducks in pond indicate some type of abuse — sexual or emotional by the parent — most often sexual.

8.   Fish in the pond — Indicates abuse by the parents.

9.   Snake next to pond — It indicates alienation of affection toward the parent.

10. Snake in pond — This indicates sexual feelings toward or a sexual relationship with the parent.

PATH SYMBOLISM: The path symbol represents the feelings the person has toward their family.

1.   Path is not connected to the house — Indicates a detached relationship with one or both of the parents.

2.   Edges of the path— If the edges are not smooth, there was rough relationship with one of the parents.

3.   Path is continuous — This indicates a good relationship with the parents.

4.   Broken path — Indicates bad feelings toward the mother or father.

5.   Flowers or other vegetation present near path — The person is trying to project an idea that the relationship with the parent is better than it really is or was.

6.   Mailbox by path — Indicates a desire to communicate with the parent. If the flag is up they have a message for the parent. If the flag is down, they would like their parent to have a message for them.

7.   Snake in path — This indicates sexual feelings or a sexual relationship with the parent.

OTHER SNAKE SYMBOLOGY REPRESENTING SEX:

1.   Snake coiled up — This represents the fear of sex or guilt associated with sex.

2.   Snake hiding in grass or flowers — Fear of past sexual experiences coming to light.

NINE ITEM SYMBOLIC PROFILE

Name _____

Sex _____

Date _____

Age _____

Directions: Draw a picture to include each of the following.

1. House   2. Snake   3. Tree   4. Pond   5. Path   6. Road   7. Fence   8. Person   9. Rainbow

PROBLEM AREAS SHEET

Name_____   Date_____

Sex_____   Age_____

INSTRUCTIONS:

I.   List the negative responses evident in the Ruth Fry Symbolic Profile, the Family Portrait, and the Nine Item Symbolic Profile on the "Problem Areas" listing.

II.   List the good or positive responses in the Ruth Fry Symbolic Profile, the Family Portrait, and the Nine Item Symbolic Profile on the "Good Things to Bring Out in Therapy" listing.

III.   Use the person's "Problem Areas" responses to treat the problems brought out in the sentence completions and pictures.

IV.   At the end of each session, discuss with the person one of the person's responses in the Good Things to Bring Out in Therapy." The person will enjoy talking about what they like or love, which will help them to think about something else other than the problems they are facing. In doing so it will help encourage them to come back for more therapy, since they enjoy talking about what the like or love.

PROBLEM AREAS:

1.

2.

3.

4.

5.

6.

7.

8.

9.

PROBLEM AREAS SHEET

GOOD THINGS TO BRING OUT IN THERAPY:

1.

2.

3.

4.

5.

6.

7.

8.

9.

10.

11.

12.

BIBLIOGRAPHY OF REFERENCES

1.   Fry, Ruth Thacker. *The Symbolic Profile*. Gulf Publishing Company, 1976.

2.   Kite, Lewis D.. *A Guide to Art Therapy.* Houston, Texas, 1998.

3.   Kouguell, M.. *DAPTH: Assessing the Unconscious in the Practice of Hypnotherapy and Counseling*. Baldwin, New York, 1994.

www.ingramcontent.com/pod-product-compliance
Lightning Source LLC
Chambersburg PA
CBHW080633030426
42336CB00018B/3183